The UNITED STATES PRESIDENTS

 James

MONROE

Megan M. Gunderson

Big Buddy Books
An Imprint of Abdo Publishing
abdopublishing.com

abdopublishing.com

Published by Abdo Publishing, a division of ABDO, PO Box 398166, Minneapolis, Minnesota 55439.
Copyright © 2017 by Abdo Consulting Group, Inc. International copyrights reserved in all countries. No part of this book may be reproduced in any form without written permission from the publisher. Big Buddy Books™ is a trademark and logo of Abdo Publishing.

Printed in the United States of America, North Mankato, Minnesota
062016
092016

THIS BOOK CONTAINS
RECYCLED MATERIALS

Design: Sarah DeYoung, Mighty Media, Inc.
Production: Mighty Media, Inc.
Editor: Rebecca Felix
Cover Photograph: Corbis
Interior Photographs: Alamy (pp. 11, 19); AP Images (pp. 5, 15); Corbis (p. 9); Getty Images (pp. 7, 23, 25); iStockphoto (pp. 7, 29); National Archives (p. 27); Photo Researchers (p. 13); Picture History (pp. 6, 17, 21)

Cataloging-in-Publication Data

Names: Gunderson, Megan M., author.
Title: James Monroe / by Megan M. Gunderson.
Description: Minneapolis, MN : Abdo Publishing, [2017] | Series: United States presidents | Includes bibliographical references and index.
Identifiers: LCCN 2015957497 | ISBN 9781680781090 (lib. bdg.) | ISBN 9781680775297 (ebook)
Subjects: LCSH: Monroe, James, 1758-1831--Juvenile literature. | Presidents--United States--Biography--Juvenile literature. | United States--Politics and government--1817-1825--Juvenile literature.
Classification: DDC 973.5/4092 [B]--dc23
LC record available at http://lccn.loc.gov/2015957497

Contents

James Monroe

James Monroe was the fifth president of the United States. He grew up in Virginia. He had a long **political** career before taking office.

Before becoming president, Monroe was governor of Virginia. Then, he became **secretary of state**. He also served as **secretary of war**.

In 1816, Monroe was elected president. He had a successful presidency. His time in office became known as the Era of Good Feelings. Today, Monroe is most remembered for the Monroe **Doctrine**.

Timeline

1758

On April 28, James Monroe was born in Westmoreland County, Virginia.

1799

Monroe was elected governor of Virginia.

1790

Monroe was elected to the US Senate.

LOUISIANA PURCHASE, 1803

1803

In France, Monroe signed the **Louisiana Purchase**.

1823

On December 2,
Monroe gave
a speech.
It **outlined** the
Monroe **Doctrine**.

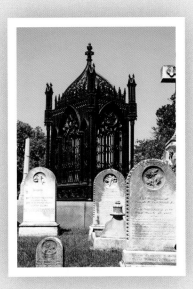

1816

Monroe was
elected the fifth
president of the
United States.

1831

On July 4, James
Monroe died.

7

Virginia Childhood

James Monroe was born in Westmoreland County, Virginia, on April 28, 1758. At that time, Virginia was a British **colony**.

At age 11, James began attending school. In 1774, he began college in Williamsburg, Virginia.

James attended the College of William and Mary in Williamsburg. At the time, Williamsburg was the capital of Virginia.

Joining the Fight

At college, Monroe listened to people speaking out against British rule. He agreed that the **colonies** should break free from Britain.

In 1775, the **American Revolution** began. Monroe wanted to join the fight. So in 1776, he left college to join the Continental army.

Meanwhile, colonial leaders signed the Declaration of Independence on July 4, 1776. It stated the colonies were free. However, official separation from Britain would only be won through years of war.

The American Revolution began with the Battles of Lexington and Concord on April 19, 1775.

In autumn 1776, Monroe fought in battles in New York. Then, on December 25, he crossed the icy Delaware River with General George Washington. This famous crossing led to the Battle of Trenton in New Jersey.

Monroe was wounded during the Battle of Trenton. He nearly died. After healing, Monroe continued to serve under Washington.

In summer 1778, Monroe served as Washington's scout in New Jersey. Soon afterward, Monroe left the military. He then returned to Williamsburg.

For his
bravery in
the Battle
of Trenton,
Monroe was
made a captain.

Politics and Family

In 1780, Monroe studied law under Virginia governor Thomas Jefferson. Monroe helped Jefferson write laws about settling America's western lands. Twice, Monroe traveled to see these areas.

Monroe was elected to the Virginia House of **Delegates** in 1782. He began serving in the Continental Congress in

Thomas Jefferson was Monroe's good friend. He worked with Monroe for many years.

1783. This group served as the US government until 1789.

While serving in Congress, Monroe met Elizabeth Kortright of New York City. They married on February 16, 1786.

The Monroes had two daughters, Eliza Kortright and Maria Hester. The Monroes' son, John Spence, died very young.

In 1786, Monroe left Congress. He began practicing law. Monroe was reelected to the Virginia House of **Delegates** in 1787.

★ DID YOU KNOW? ★

Monroe held more elected public offices than any other US president.

Monroe and
his new wife,
Elizabeth, moved
to Fredericksburg,
Virginia, in 1786.

Foreign Relations

In 1789, George Washington became president. Monroe was elected to the US Senate in 1790. Soon after, Britain and France went to war.

Some US **politicians** sided with Britain. Washington feared this would hurt America's **relations** with France. He named Monroe **minister** to France to avoid this.

Washington felt Monroe did not **represent** his country well in France. He asked Monroe to return home. Monroe returned in 1797. He then wrote a **pamphlet** attacking Washington.

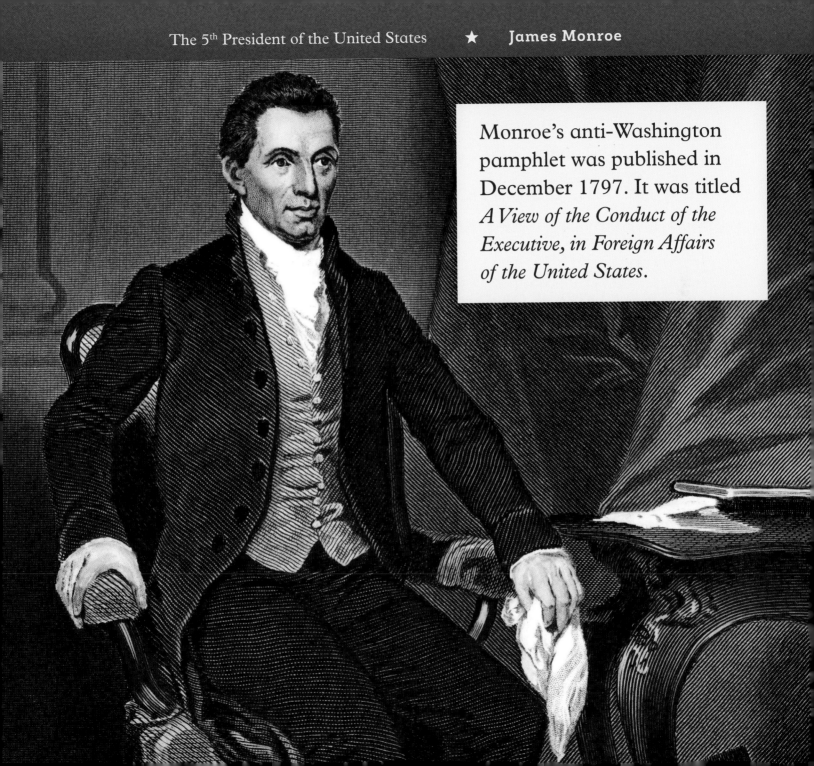

Monroe's anti-Washington pamphlet was published in December 1797. It was titled *A View of the Conduct of the Executive, in Foreign Affairs of the United States.*

In 1799, Monroe was elected governor of Virginia. In 1801, Thomas Jefferson became president. He sent Monroe back to France in January 1803.

The United States wanted to purchase New Orleans from France. This area of Louisiana was important to US trade. On May 2, Monroe signed the **Louisiana Purchase**. It doubled the size of the United States.

Meanwhile, Monroe was named **minister** to Great Britain. Around this time, the British had been attacking US ships. In July, Monroe went to London. There, the two sides signed a **treaty** in 1806. But Jefferson did not agree to it.

The signing of the Louisiana Purchase

LOUISIANA PURCHASE, 1803

Secretary of State

In 1811, Monroe became **secretary of state**. Meanwhile, Britain continued attacking US ships. On June 18, 1812, Congress declared war on Britain, starting the **War of 1812**.

Monroe was named **secretary of war** in September 1814. Now, he held two **cabinet** positions at once!

The United States and Britain agreed to end the war in December. Many people were happy with Monroe's leadership during the war. In 1816, he ran for president and won.

Daniel D. Tompkins served as Monroe's vice president.

President Monroe

Monroe became president on March 4, 1817. When he took office, there was trouble on the border between Georgia and Florida. At this time, Spain controlled Florida. Runaway slaves and Native Americans from Florida were attacking US towns in Georgia.

Monroe sent an army to Florida to stop the attacks. **Secretary of State** John Quincy Adams then crafted an agreement with Spain. In it, Spain gave Florida to the United States.

PRESIDENT MONROE'S CABINET

First Term
March 4, 1817–March 5, 1821

★ **STATE:** John Quincy Adams
★ **TREASURY:** William H. Crawford
★ **WAR:** John C. Calhoun
★ **NAVY:** Benjamin W. Crowninshield, Smith Thompson (from January 1, 1819)
★ **ATTORNEY GENERAL:** Richard Rush, William Wirt (from November 15, 1817

Second Term
March 5, 1821–March 4, 1825

★ **STATE:** John Quincy Adams
★ **TREASURY:** William H. Crawford
★ **WAR:** John C. Calhoun
★ **NAVY:** Smith Thompson, Samuel L. Southard (from September 16, 1823)
★ **ATTORNEY GENERAL:** William Wirt

25

In 1820, Monroe was reelected president. On December 2, 1823, he gave a famous speech. It **outlined** what would become the Monroe **Doctrine**.

At the time, the United States feared Europe would try to take back some **colonies** or create new ones. In his speech, Monroe said North and South America were free. Europe should not try to set up new colonies there.

The Monroe Doctrine is a very important part of Monroe's presidency. Long after he left office, US presidents continued to follow its ideas.

★ SUPREME COURT APPOINTMENTS ★

Smith Thompson: 1823

The Monroe Doctrine came from the president's seventh annual address to Congress.

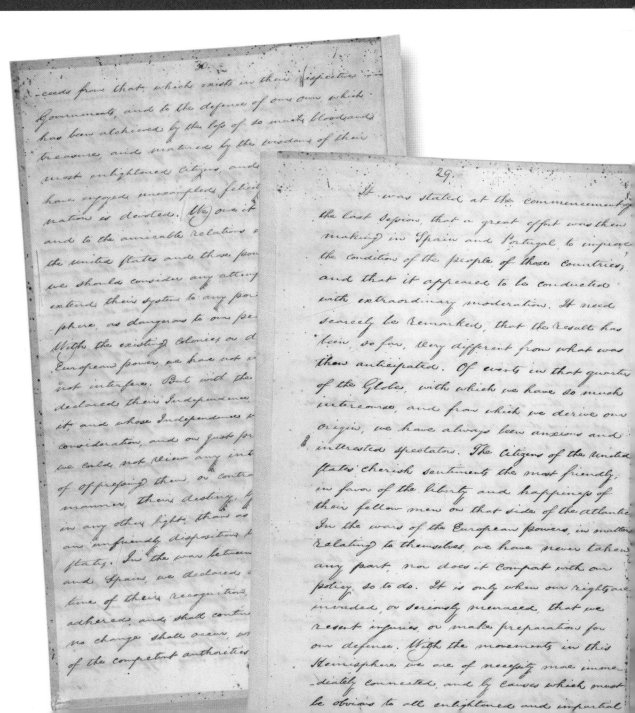

Going Home

President Monroe decided not to run for a third term. In 1825, he **retired**. The Monroes moved to Leesburg, Virginia.

In 1830, Monroe's wife died. Monroe moved to New York City. Meanwhile, his health weakened. Monroe died on July 4, 1831.

James Monroe was successful in **politics**. He helped with foreign **relations**. And, he **outlined** the Monroe **Doctrine**. Monroe's work had a lasting effect on the United States.

Monroe's
grave site
in Richmond,
Virginia

Office of the President

Branches of Government

The US government has three branches. They are the executive, legislative, and judicial branches. Each branch has some power over the others. This is called a system of checks and balances.

★ Executive Branch

The executive branch enforces laws. It is made up of the president, the vice president, and the president's cabinet. The president represents the United States around the world. He or she also signs bills into law and leads the military.

★ Legislative Branch

The legislative branch makes laws, maintains the military, and regulates trade. It also has the power to declare war. This branch includes the Senate and the House of Representatives. Together, these two houses form Congress.

★ Judicial Branch

The judicial branch interprets laws. It is made up of district courts, courts of appeals, and the Supreme Court. District courts try cases. Sometimes people disagree with a trial's outcome. Then he or she may appeal. If a court of appeals supports the ruling, a person may appeal to the Supreme Court.

Qualifications for Office

To be president, a candidate must be at least 35 years old. The person must be a natural-born US citizen. He or she must also have lived in the United States for at least 14 years.

Electoral College

The US presidential election is an indirect election. Voters from each state choose electors. These electors represent their state in the Electoral College. Each elector has one electoral vote. Electors cast their vote for the candidate with the highest number of votes from people in their state. A candidate must receive the majority of Electoral College votes to win.

Term of Office

Each president may be elected to two four-year terms. The presidential election is held on the Tuesday after the first Monday in November. The president is sworn in on January 20 of the following year. At that time, he or she takes the oath of office.
It states:

> I do solemnly swear (or affirm) that I will faithfully execute the office of President of the United States, and will to the best of my ability, preserve, protect and defend the Constitution of the United States.

31

Line of Succession

The Presidential Succession Act of 1947 states who becomes president if the president cannot serve. The vice president is first in the line. Next are the Speaker of the House and the President Pro Tempore of the Senate. It may happen that none of these individuals is able to serve. Then the office falls to the president's cabinet members. They would take office in the order in which each department was created:

Secretary of State

Secretary of the Treasury

Secretary of Defense

Attorney General

Secretary of the Interior

Secretary of Agriculture

Secretary of Commerce

Secretary of Labor

Secretary of Health and Human Services

Secretary of Housing and Urban Development

Secretary of Transportation

Secretary of Energy

Secretary of Education

Secretary of Veterans Affairs

Secretary of Homeland Security

Benefits

★ While in office, the president receives a salary. It is $400,000 per year. He or she lives in the White House. The president also has 24-hour Secret Service protection.

★ The president may travel on a Boeing 747 jet. This special jet is called Air Force One. It can hold 70 passengers. It has kitchens, a dining room, sleeping areas, and more. Air Force One can fly halfway around the world before needing to refuel. It can even refuel in flight!

★ When the president travels by car, he or she uses Cadillac One. It is a Cadillac Deville that has been modified. The car has heavy armor and communications systems. The president may even take Cadillac One along when visiting other countries.

★ The president also travels on a helicopter. It is called Marine One. It may also be taken along when the president visits other countries.

★ Sometimes the president needs to get away with family and friends. Camp David is the official presidential retreat. It is located in Maryland. The US Navy maintains the retreat. The US Marine Corps keeps it secure. The camp offers swimming, tennis, golf, and hiking.

★ When the president leaves office, he or she receives lifetime Secret Service protection. He or she also receives a yearly pension of $203,700. The former president also receives money for office space, supplies, and staff.

PRESIDENTS AND THEIR TERMS

PRESIDENT	PARTY	TOOK OFFICE	LEFT OFFICE	TERMS SERVED	VICE PRESIDENT
George Washington	None	April 30, 1789	March 4, 1797	Two	John Adams
John Adams	Federalist	March 4, 1797	March 4, 1801	One	Thomas Jefferson
Thomas Jefferson	Democratic-Republican	March 4, 1801	March 4, 1809	Two	Aaron Burr, George Clinton
James Madison	Democratic-Republican	March 4, 1809	March 4, 1817	Two	George Clinton, Elbridge Gerry
James Monroe	Democratic-Republican	March 4, 1817	March 4, 1825	Two	Daniel D. Tompkins
John Quincy Adams	Democratic-Republican	March 4, 1825	March 4, 1829	One	John C. Calhoun
Andrew Jackson	Democrat	March 4, 1829	March 4, 1837	Two	John C. Calhoun, Martin Van Buren
Martin Van Buren	Democrat	March 4, 1837	March 4, 1841	One	Richard M. Johnson
William H. Harrison	Whig	March 4, 1841	April 4, 1841	Died During First Term	John Tyler
John Tyler	Whig	April 6, 1841	March 4, 1845	Completed Harrison's Term	Office Vacant
James K. Polk	Democrat	March 4, 1845	March 4, 1849	One	George M. Dallas
Zachary Taylor	Whig	March 5, 1849	July 9, 1850	Died During First Term	Millard Fillmore

PRESIDENT	PARTY	TOOK OFFICE	LEFT OFFICE	TERMS SERVED	VICE PRESIDENT
Millard Fillmore	Whig	July 10, 1850	March 4, 1853	Completed Taylor's Term	Office Vacant
Franklin Pierce	Democrat	March 4, 1853	March 4, 1857	One	William R.D. King
James Buchanan	Democrat	March 4, 1857	March 4, 1861	One	John C. Breckinridge
Abraham Lincoln	Republican	March 4, 1861	April 15, 1865	Served One Term, Died During Second Term	Hannibal Hamlin, Andrew Johnson
Andrew Johnson	Democrat	April 15, 1865	March 4, 1869	Completed Lincoln's Second Term	Office Vacant
Ulysses S. Grant	Republican	March 4, 1869	March 4, 1877	Two	Schuyler Colfax, Henry Wilson
Rutherford B. Hayes	Republican	March 3, 1877	March 4, 1881	One	William A. Wheeler
James A. Garfield	Republican	March 4, 1881	September 19, 1881	Died During First Term	Chester Arthur
Chester Arthur	Republican	September 20, 1881	March 4, 1885	Completed Garfield's Term	Office Vacant
Grover Cleveland	Democrat	March 4, 1885	March 4, 1889	One	Thomas A. Hendricks
Benjamin Harrison	Republican	March 4, 1889	March 4, 1893	One	Levi P. Morton
Grover Cleveland	Democrat	March 4, 1893	March 4, 1897	One	Adlai E. Stevenson
William McKinley	Republican	March 4, 1897	September 14, 1901	Served One Term, Died During Second Term	Garret A. Hobart, Theodore Roosevelt

PRESIDENT	PARTY	TOOK OFFICE	LEFT OFFICE	TERMS SERVED	VICE PRESIDENT
Theodore Roosevelt	Republican	September 14, 1901	March 4, 1909	Completed McKinley's Second Term, Served One Term	Office Vacant, Charles Fairbanks
William Taft	Republican	March 4, 1909	March 4, 1913	One	James S. Sherman
Woodrow Wilson	Democrat	March 4, 1913	March 4, 1921	Two	Thomas R. Marshall
Warren G. Harding	Republican	March 4, 1921	August 2, 1923	Died During First Term	Calvin Coolidge
Calvin Coolidge	Republican	August 3, 1923	March 4, 1929	Completed Harding's Term, Served One Term	Office Vacant, Charles Dawes
Herbert Hoover	Republican	March 4, 1929	March 4, 1933	One	Charles Curtis
Franklin D. Roosevelt	Democrat	March 4, 1933	April 12, 1945	Served Three Terms, Died During Fourth Term	John Nance Garner, Henry A. Wallace, Harry S. Truman
Harry S. Truman	Democrat	April 12, 1945	January 20, 1953	Completed Roosevelt's Fourth Term, Served One Term	Office Vacant, Alben Barkley
Dwight D. Eisenhower	Republican	January 20, 1953	January 20, 1961	Two	Richard Nixon
John F. Kennedy	Democrat	January 20, 1961	November 22, 1963	Died During First Term	Lyndon B. Johnson
Lyndon B. Johnson	Democrat	November 22, 1963	January 20, 1969	Completed Kennedy's Term, Served One Term	Office Vacant, Hubert H. Humphrey
Richard Nixon	Republican	January 20, 1969	August 9, 1974	Completed First Term, Resigned During Second Term	Spiro T. Agnew, Gerald Ford

PRESIDENT	PARTY	TOOK OFFICE	LEFT OFFICE	TERMS SERVED	VICE PRESIDENT
Gerald Ford	Republican	August 9, 1974	January 20, 1977	Completed Nixon's Second Term	Nelson A. Rockefeller
Jimmy Carter	Democrat	January 20, 1977	January 20, 1981	One	Walter Mondale
Ronald Reagan	Republican	January 20, 1981	January 20, 1989	Two	George H.W. Bush
George H.W. Bush	Republican	January 20, 1989	January 20, 1993	One	Dan Quayle
Bill Clinton	Democrat	January 20, 1993	January 20, 2001	Two	Al Gore
George W. Bush	Republican	January 20, 2001	January 20, 2009	Two	Dick Cheney
Barack Obama	Democrat	January 20, 2009	January 20, 2017	Two	Joe Biden

"Peace is the best time for improvement and preparation of every kind."

James Monroe

★ WRITE TO THE PRESIDENT ★

You may write to the president at:
The White House
1600 Pennsylvania Avenue NW
Washington, DC 20500

You may e-mail the president at:
comments@whitehouse.gov

37

Glossary

American Revolution—the war between Americans and the British from 1775 to 1783. The Americans won their freedom from the British.

cabinet—a group of advisers chosen by the president to lead government departments.

colony—land settled by people from another area.

delegate—someone who represents other people at a meeting or in a lawmaking group.

doctrine—a statement that frames a government plan.

Louisiana Purchase—land the United States purchased from France in 1803. It extended from the Mississippi River to the Rocky Mountains and from Canada through the Gulf of Mexico.

minister—a type of government official.

outline—to give a brief description of the main points.

pamphlet—a small, thin book of papers with information about a certain subject.

politics—the art or science of government. Something referring to politics is political. A person who is active in politics is a politician.

relations—the ways in which two or more people, groups, or countries talk to, behave toward, and deal with each other.

represent—to officially speak or act for a person, group, state, or country.

retire—to give up one's job.

secretary of state—a member of the president's cabinet who handles relations with other countries.

secretary of war—a member of the president's cabinet who handled the military and national defense.

treaty—an agreement made between two or more groups.

War of 1812—a war between the United States and England from 1812 to 1815.

★ WEBSITES ★

To learn more about the US Presidents, visit **booklinks.abdopublishing.com**. These links are routinely monitored and updated to provide the most current information available.

Index